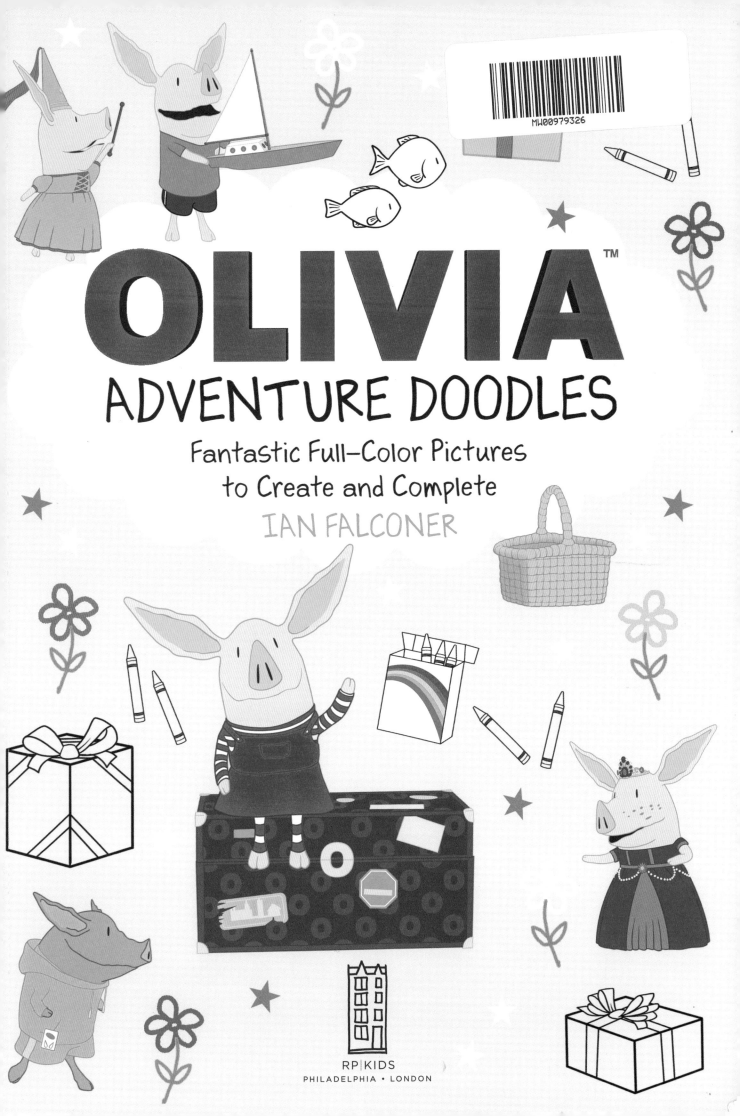

OLIVIA™
ADVENTURE DOODLES
Fantastic Full-Color Pictures to Create and Complete

IAN FALCONER

RP|KIDS
PHILADELPHIA · LONDON

Books published by Running Press are available at special discounts for bulk purchases in the United States by
corporations, institutions, and other organizations. For more information, please contact the Special Markets
Department at the Perseus Books Group, 2300 Chestnut Street, Suite 200, Philadelphia, PA 19103,
or call (800) 810-4145, ext. 5000, or e-mail special.markets@perseusbooks.com.

ISBN 978-0-7624-5590-4

9 8 7 6 5 4 3 2 1

Digit on the right indicates the number of this printing

Designed by Sarah Pierson
Text adapted by T. L. Bonaddio
Art adapted by Tom Brannon
Edited by Marlo Scrimizzi
Typography: Olivia and Helvetica Neue

Published by Running Press Kids
An Imprint of Running Press Book Publishers
A Member of the Perseus Books Group
2300 Chestnut Street
Philadelphia, PA 19103–4371

Visit us on the web!
www.runningpress.com/kids

Set sail with Olivia!
Finish the bouncy ship.

Olivia learns to talk to turkeys!
Who pops out of the bushes?

Mrs. Hogenmuller's favorite animal is a turkey.
What's yours? Draw it on the chalkboard.

Olivia records a very special message.

Write your own special message here!

Olivia is at the beach!
What toy is she blowing up?

Oh no! Rain!
Decorate Olivia's beach umbrella.

Olivia imagines hiking a huge hill.
Help her catch some stars!

Decorate the flag for Olivia!

Olivia can never be too prepared!
What does she pack for her hike?

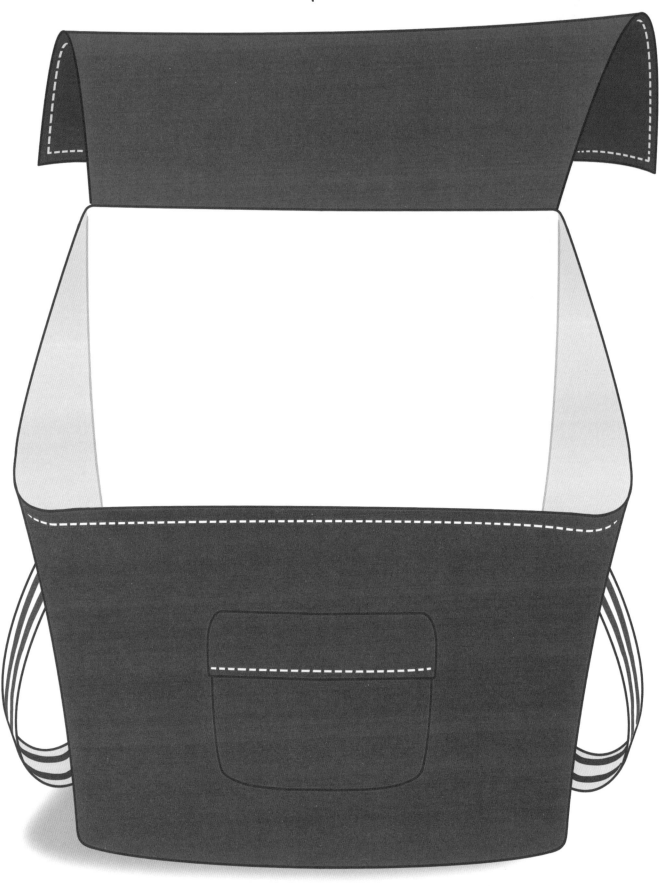

Fill Olivia's backpack.

What does Olivia's father pack in the car?

Watch out! A skunk!
How does Olivia distract the smelly skunk?

Will Olivia make it to the top of the hill?
Draw her a trail to follow.

Make a map of your own adventure!

Design Olivia a sled to slide through the snow!

Complete Olivia and Ian's cotton-candy creations.

Help draw Olivia's plan to build a Snowlady!

Give the Snowlady a pretty face.

Olivia and Francine make snow angels!

Olivia and Ian twist balloons into fun shapes!
Make Olivia a balloon daisy.

Make Ian a balloon sword.

Get Well!

Oh no! Olivia fell while dancing.
Help decorate a card for her.

Design some special sticky
stickers to add to the card.

William is missing wheels on his walker!
Draw them back for him.

Collect all kinds of wheels in
Olivia's wagon for her invention.

Give Olivia and her friends
pirate hats for a party!

Olivia takes charge of party planning!
Who is she talking to on the phone?

Fill the table for a proper tea party.

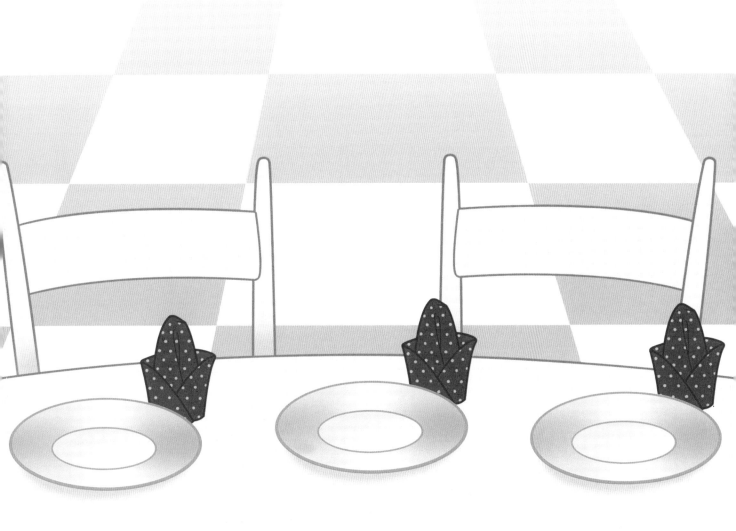

What a blowy, blustery day!

Complete Olivia's umbrella.

What is tugging on the other end
of Ian and Olivia's rope?

Add some more bows to the tail of Olivia's kite.

Decorate your own kite!

Olivia keeps a really close watch on
something very important!

Olivia's mother made cookies!

No one is allowed in the living room!

What can you draw around the piano to keep the model safe?

Olivia imagines building the perfect house.
Design your own perfectly perfect house!

There are so many boxes to recycle!
Build something big out of boxes.

Give Olivia a baton to twirl.

Meet Jasper, a real, live gold miner!
Can you draw him a bandana around his
neck and hat for his head?

Time for some grub!
Olivia and her classmates need some bowls.

Draw a horse for Olivia to pet.

What would you name your horse?
Make a list!

5 Favorite Horse Names

1.

2.

3.

4.

5.

Oh no! Mrs. Hogenmuller can't find the bus key!
Empty her bag.

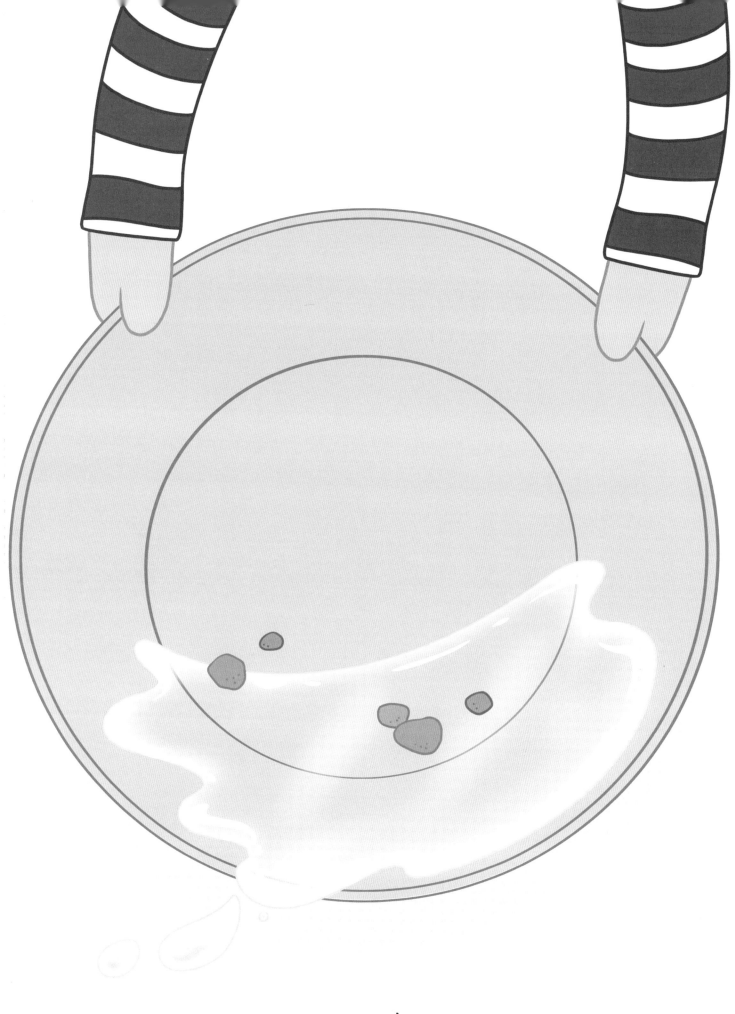

Treasure Hunt!
What does Olivia find in the pan?

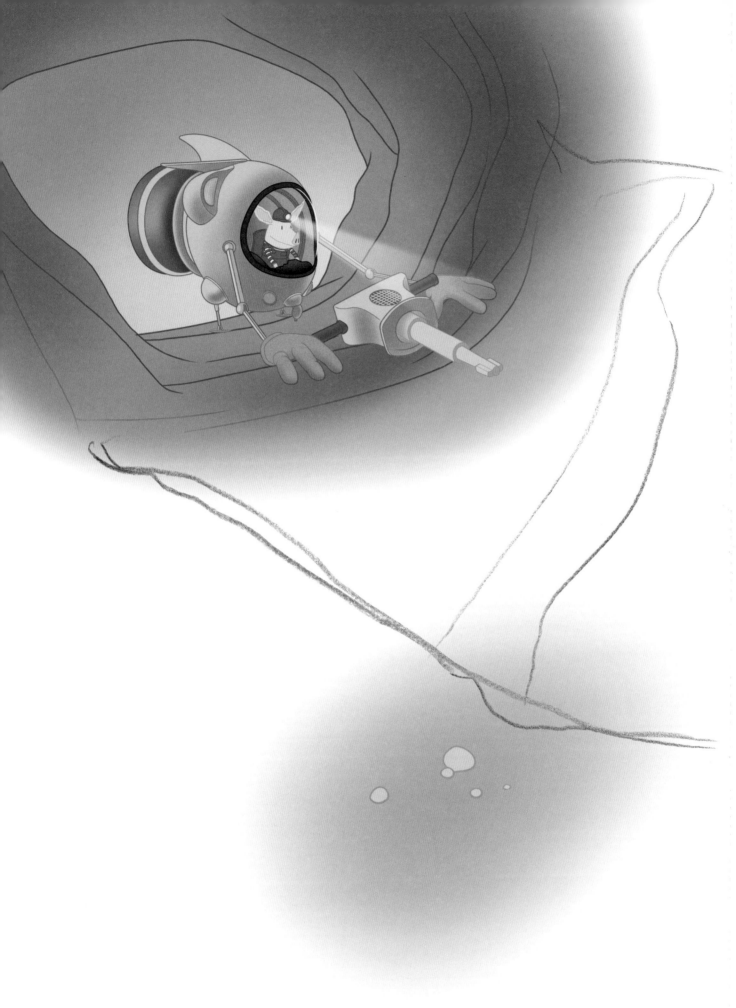

Olivia is in search of gold!
Complete the tunnel.

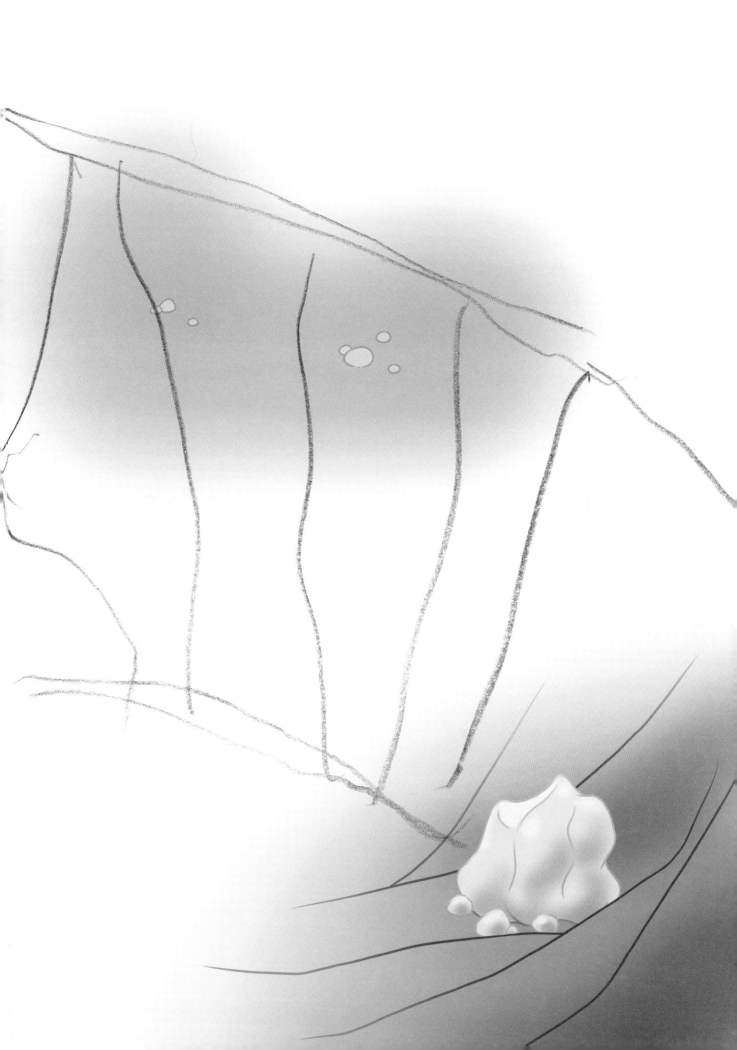

Draw a key to get Daisy out of jail.

The Mighty Olivia can make it rain!

Can you help make Francine's flowers grow?

What has Olivia's mother packed for the picnic?

Planning a wedding is fun!

Stamp and address this invitation.

Olivia needs a lot of water balloons!
Fill the page with as many as possible.

Draw William something furry
to make him stop crying.

Perry makes a new friend!

Decorate the mailbox.

Step on it!
Complete the racetrack to help
Olivia finish the race.

Olivia imagines flying an airplane under a rainbow!

Who is Olivia's copilot?

Woohoo!
Make some waves for Olivia.

Design your own surfboard.

Olivia loves to take pictures of Perry!
Capture your own pictures here.

It's such a hot day!
Draw Ian an ice pop to keep cool.

Look! It's Magnificent Magnet Girl!
Finish her outfit with a big cape.

Give the comic book store a super name!

Make your own comic book cover!

Help! A meteor!

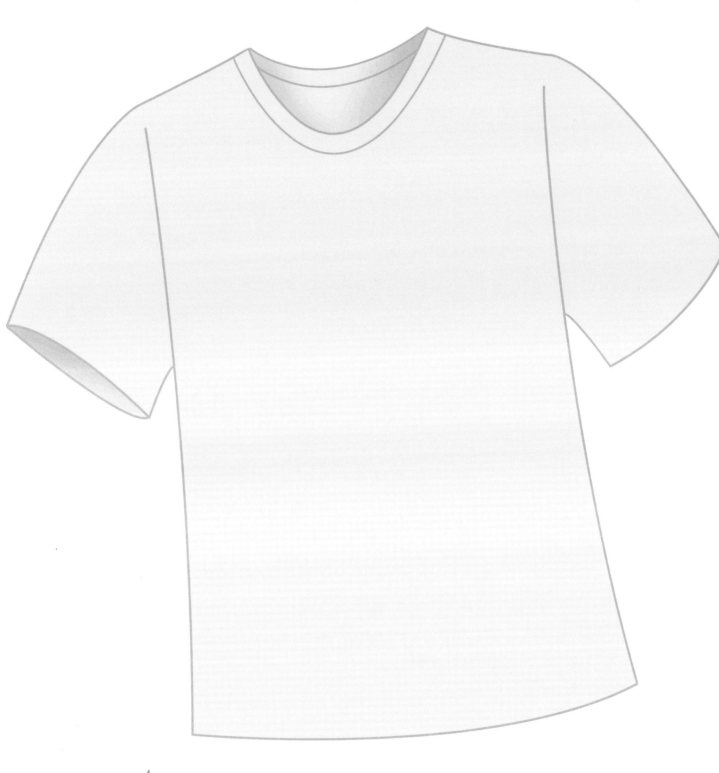

Create your own superhero logo,
like Magnificent Magnet Girl!
Draw it on the T-shirt.

Magnificent Magnet Girl's motto is
"Never Give Up, Stick with It!"
Make your own motto on the back
of the T-shirt.

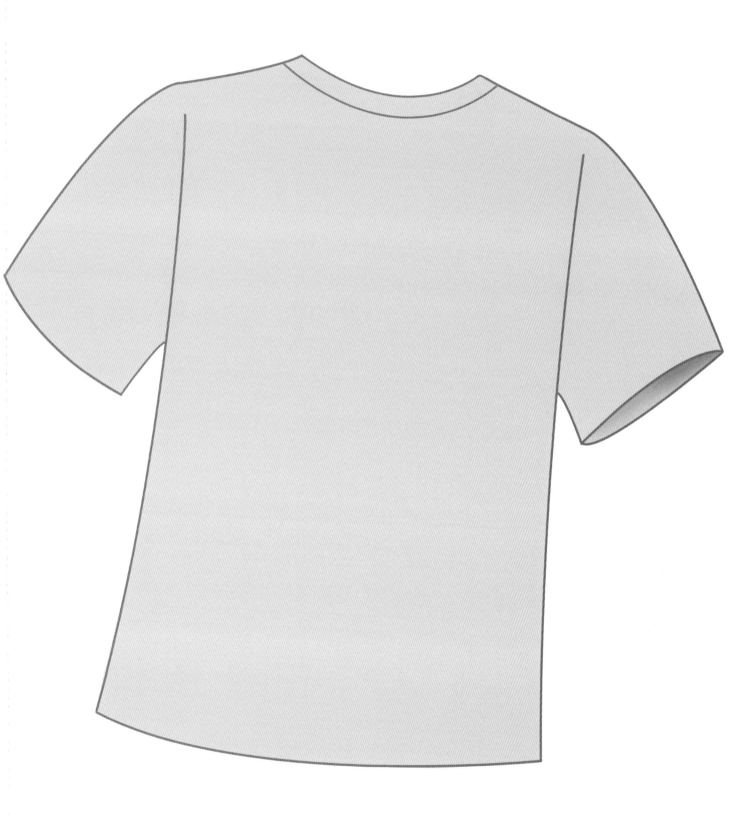

Olivia puts on a play!

Draw her a big audience.

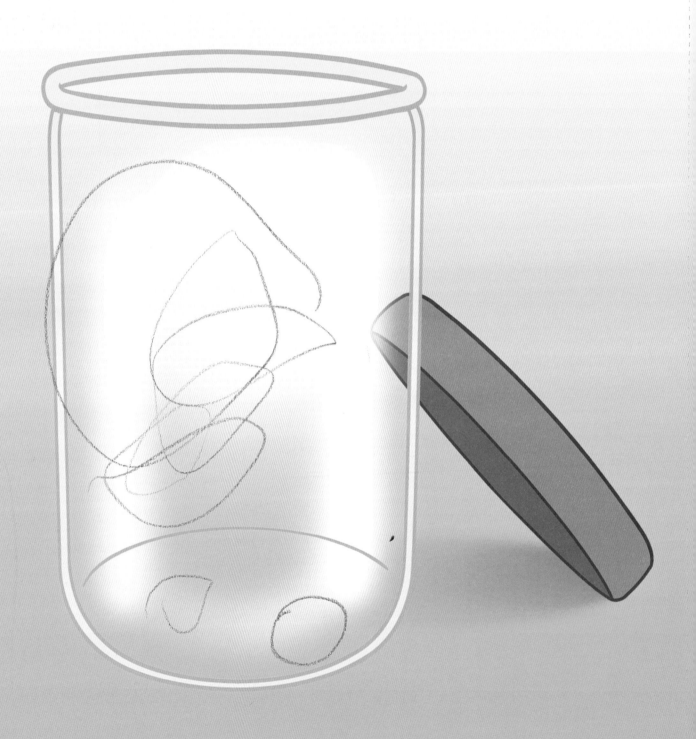

Fill the jar full of coins for Olivia.

You're the guard cat, Edwin. Stand guard!

Mirror, mirror, on the wall . . .
What does Olivia see in the mirror?

Design pretty princess dresses
for Olivia, Francine, and Daisy.

Make sure to give them magic wands!

Make your own Princess Pledge!

A Princess promises to be _____,
_____, _____, and _____, a lot,
_____ very loudly,

and never be mean ...

Every princess needs a dragon.
Draw one here!

Help fix the royal family's carriage
by drawing the wheels!

Olivia and Princess Stephanie love
Cherry Chunk ice cream!

Complete the castle.

Olivia is a princess for a day!
Color her room princess purple.

Olivia needs a stool to stand on!

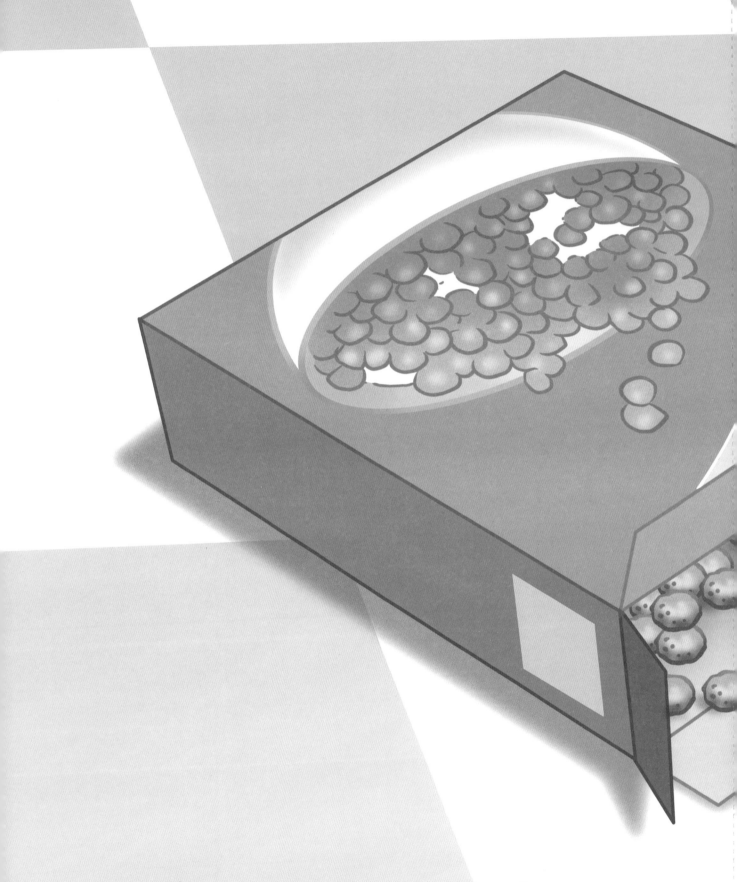

Look! What surprise does Olivia
find in the cereal box?

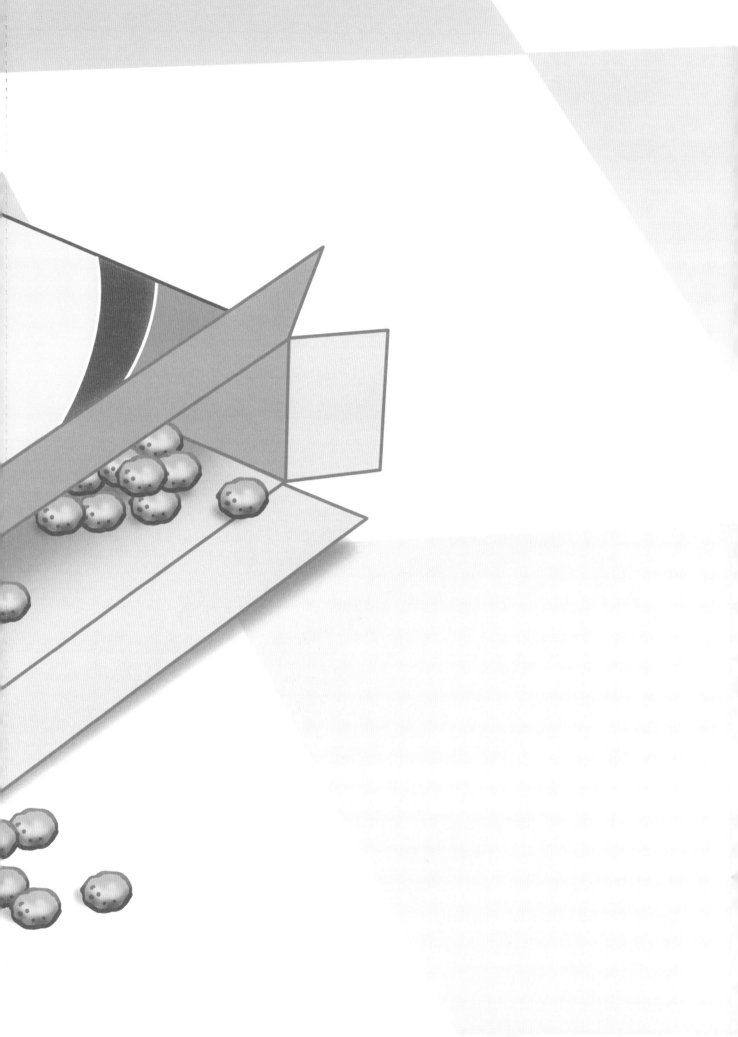

Going up!
Super, teeny-tiny Olivia saves a
charm bracelet in the sink!
Draw her a rope to get out.

Olivia finds things that remind her of Francine. What reminds you of your best friend?

Add Fizzle Berry juice to the
bowl to make pie with Olivia!

Olivia likes taking a roller-coaster ride.
Draw her some friends.

Look at the bracelet Olivia made for Francine from all of their adventures!

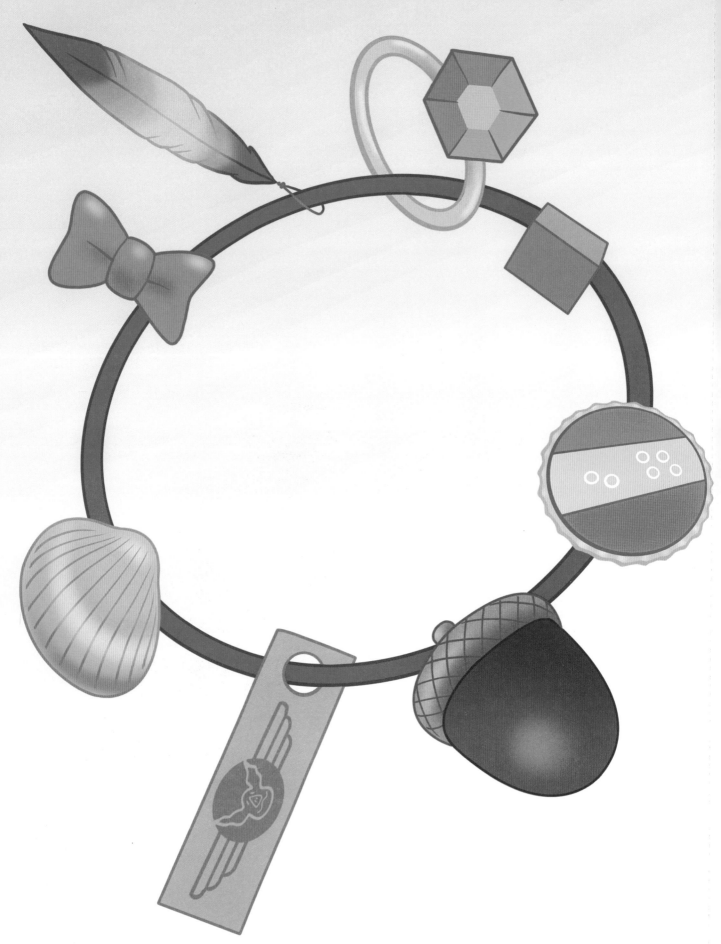

Design your own bracelet for a friend.

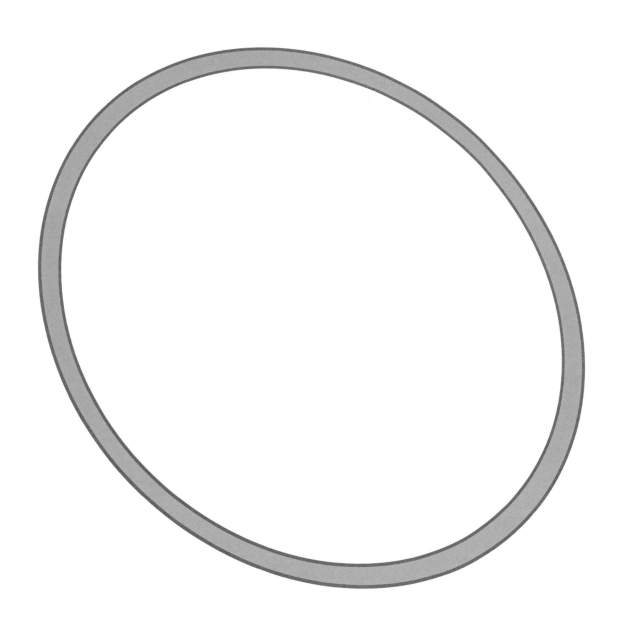

Decorate the cake for a birthday party!

Create your own secret flashlight code!

1 Flash = Hello!

2 Flashes = _____

3 Flashes = _____

4 Flashes = _____

5 Flashes = _____

What is Perry barking at in the tree?

Olivia loves to check books out of the library!

Fill the bookshelf with your favorite books.

Give Olivia some drumsticks to play.

Add spots to the fireman's dog.

Olivia catches a falling star!
Make a wish.

I wish...

Put the tail on the falling star!

Planning a vacation is so much work!
Help Olivia make a packing list
for her trip to the beach.

☑ Sunglasses
☑ Umbrella
☑ Sunscreen
☐
☐
☐
☐
☐

Look at all the colorful fish!

Olivia imagines her sandbox is a tropical island!
Add some palm trees and flamingos.

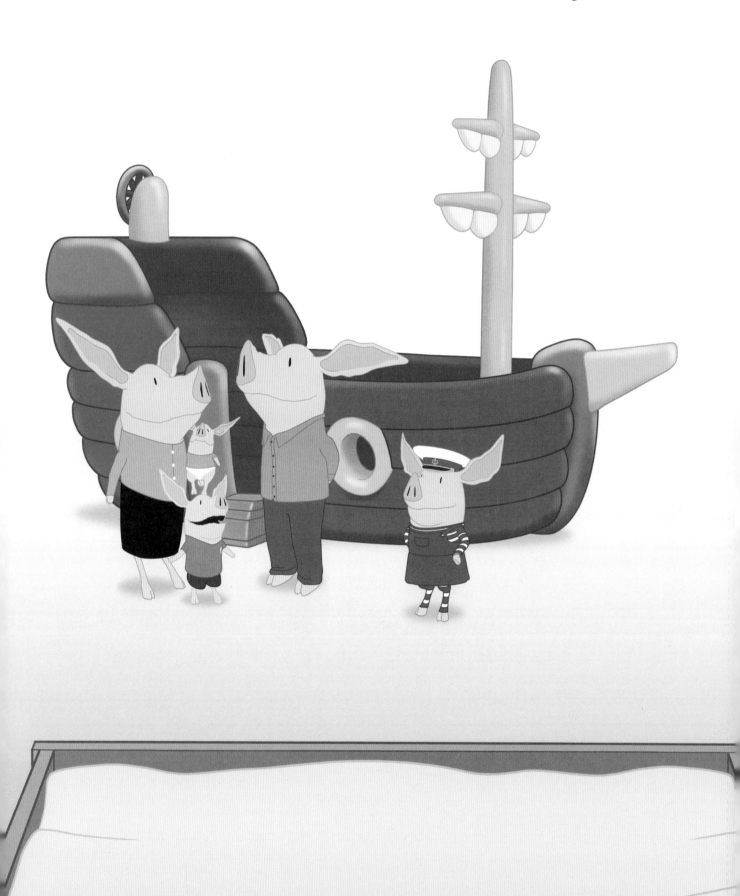

A show-and-tell superstar!

Draw some butterflies for
Olivia and Francine to catch.

There's still so much to do!
What's on Olivia's mind before she goes to sleep?